Bugs Up Close

Written by
Diane Swanson

Photographed by
Paul Davidson

Kids Can Press

To Carolyn, whose early fascination with bugs reignited mine — DS
To Jera — PD

Acknowledgments

The author greatly appreciates the editorial talents of Val Wyatt, the design creativity of Julia Naimska, the fabulous photography of Paul Davidson and the entomological expertise of Dr. Richard Ring, Professor Emeritus, University of Victoria. Dr. Ring is President of the Entomological Society of BC, Editor-in-Chief of *The Canadian Entomologist* and the 2006 recipient of the Entomological Society of Canada's Gold Medal for Outstanding Achievement in Canadian Entomology.

The photographer wishes to thank the Canadian National Collection of Insects, Agriculture and Agri-Food Canada, especially Mr. Jim Troubridge, Dr. Henri Goulet and Dr. John Huber, for their valuable help, guidance, enthusiasm and friendship. Thanks to Dr. Stephen Cumbaa, Canadian Museum of Nature. Thanks also to BugGuide.net and all the volunteers there who were willing share their love and knowledge of insects with others, and especially to Troy Bartlett, the genius behind BugGuide (http://BugGuide.net), and John VanDyk, who maintains the site for the benefit of bug lovers!

Kids Can Press acknowledges the financial support of the Government of Ontario, through the Ontario Media Development Corporation's Ontario Book Initiative; the Ontario Arts Council; the Canada Council for the Arts; and the Government of Canada, through the BPIDP, for our publishing activity.

Published in Canada by
Kids Can Press Ltd.
29 Birch Avenue
Toronto, ON M4V 1E2

Published in the U.S. by
Kids Can Press Ltd.
2250 Military Road
Tonawanda, NY 14150

www.kidscanpress.com

Edited by Valerie Wyatt
Designed by Julia Naimska
Printed and bound in Singapore

The hardcover edition of this book is smyth sewn casebound.
The paperback edition of this book is limp sewn with a drawn-on cover.

CM 07 0 9 8 7 6 5 4 3 2 1
CM PA 07 0 9 8 7 6 5 4 3 2 1

Library and Archives Canada Cataloguing in Publication

Swanson, Diane, 1944–
Bugs up close / written by Diane Swanson.

Includes index.
ISBN 978-1-55453-138-7 (bound). ISBN 978-1-55453-139-4 (pbk.)

1. Insects—Juvenile literature. I. Title.

QL467.2.S9625 2007   j595.7   C2006-906852-6

Kids Can Press is a *Corus*™ Entertainment company

Contents

Insects

You are sitting under a tree when something tickles your toes. You brush it off, and the tiny critter crawls away through the grass. Then you notice a green bug hopping by and see yellow wings fluttering above your head.

Creeping, jumping, flying — little creatures seem to be everywhere. But not all of them are insects. The insects are the ones that have three main body sections. Most insects also have antennae, wings and six legs (three on each side).

Look at this picture of a flower fly. You can see three separate body sections and three legs along one side of its body. It has wings, too, and short antennae on its head. The flower fly IS an insect.

Buggy Bit

The flower fly is an insect. The daddy longlegs and spider are not insects.

The daddy longlegs and the spider are NOT insects. The daddy longlegs has only one main body section, and the spider has just two. They each have more than six legs. Neither of them has wings or antennae.

Insect or not? Sometimes you have to look closely to tell.

Daddy longlegs

Spider

Flower fly

Bodies

Notice the three main sections in the body of this wasp. Like other insects, it has a head, a thorax (middle section) and an abdomen (rear section). On some insects, it is hard to tell where the thorax ends and the abdomen begins. A covering that overlaps them can make the two sections look like one.

The head is where you will find the eyes, mouthparts and usually antennae. A short neck often joins the head to the thorax.

The thorax has six legs attached to it, three on each side. Many insects also have wings on their thorax. And there may be openings that are used for breathing.

The abdomen is usually where most of the insect's breathing openings are found. Special parts, such as stingers, are sometimes attached to the abdomen, too.

Weird looking? You bet. But insect bodies are designed to help bugs survive.

A narrow "waist" makes it possible for a wasp to turn around in tight spaces, such as inside a nest.

Wasp

Exoskeletons

Unlike you, an insect has no bones. Instead, it has a strong outer covering called an exoskeleton. This covering supports many of the insect's muscles. It also protects the insides of the insect from injury.

The exoskeleton, like the one on this blow fly, is made of separate plates. Soft, flexible material between the plates allows the insect to expand as it feeds and to bend its legs when it walks. A thin, waxy layer in the exoskeleton prevents the insect from drying out.

An insect grows, but its exoskeleton doesn't. When the covering becomes too tight, the insect molts (sheds its exoskeleton). Many insects molt five or six times during their lives, but some molt more than fifty times.

As an insect molts, it exposes the larger, softer exoskeleton that has formed beneath the old one. The insect is at risk from weather and predators until this new covering hardens.

Exoskeletons may be dull or shiny, drab or brightly colored. They may be thick or thin, smooth or bumpy, spiny or hairy.

Buggy Bit
The exoskeleton of a fly is thin but tough.

Blow fly

Spiracles

Insects don't have lungs like you do. Instead, many of them breathe in air through tiny openings called spiracles [SPY-rah-kulz]. The spiracles lead to tubes that carry the air throughout the insects' bodies.

An insect may have as many as four spiracles on its thorax and sixteen on its abdomen.

Spiracles vary a lot in size and shape, but most contain hairs that filter out dust. Many insects can close their spiracles, which helps prevent their bodies from drying out. If an insect loses too much moisture, it will die.

Air sometimes moves in and out of the same spiracles, but it often goes in one spiracle and out another. The spiracles that are open control the way the air flows.

The damselfly has spiracles on its abdomen and thorax. They're so tiny that you can't even see them in this picture.

Damselfly

Buggy Bit

Damselflies don't have spiracles until they become adults, like the one here. Young damselflies live in water and breathe through gills.

Legs

Monarch butterfly

ost insects have six legs. The front and back legs on one side often step with the middle leg on the other side. The remaining three legs take the next step. This way of walking, plus all the joints in their legs, helps insects travel smoothly, even over bumpy ground. That's how the boxelder bug in the picture can move easily over an uneven surface.

Insect legs usually end in a pair of claws that can grip rough things, such as tree bark. Between the claws are often one or two sacs that may be very sticky. The sacs help insects cross smooth surfaces, such as windows.

But for many insects, legs are more than walking tools. Grasshoppers, for instance, have large, powerful back legs for jumping. In a single leap, they can cover a distance fifteen times the length of their bodies. And dung beetles, among others, use their front legs like shovels to dig through soil.

The praying mantis and monarch butterfly on these pages have different uses for legs. The large front legs of the praying mantis can move lightning fast to seize its prey. The butterfly tastes with the tips of some of its legs. When it finds something sweet, it sucks up the food.

Boxelder bug

Praying mantis

Wings

Insects were the first animals to fly, and most are SUPER fliers. They dart forward, backward and sideways. Many can even hover in the air like tiny helicopters. And they move fast. Blow flies can travel 300 times their body length in one second.

A few insects have no wings. Other insects have two wings, but many have four. Often all the wings are used for flying, but in some four-winged insects, one pair may have a special use. A ladybug's front wings, for example, serve as wing covers. A fly's tiny back wings help the insect balance.

Insect wings are made of thin material strengthened by a mass of crisscrossing veins. Check out the veins in the mayfly's wings.

Thousands of overlapping scales cover the wings of insects such as butterflies and moths. The scales make wings stronger and give them color. They also absorb heat from the Sun and help keep the insect warm.

Buggy Bit

A mayfly holds its wings up when it rests.

Moth wing up close

Most insects can spread their wings and gl-i-de. But to fly, they must beat their wings, down and forward, up and backward. How rapidly insects beat their wings varies a lot. In one second, a big butterfly may flap only 8 times, while a mosquito will flap 600 times. Some small flies flap 1000 times a second. Insects can flap so fast you can barely see their wings. But you can hear them. Just listen for the high-pitched buzzzzzzz.

Mayfly

Mouthparts

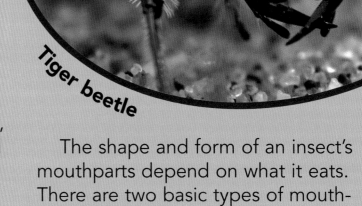

Tiger beetle

Imagine having your jaws and teeth outside — not inside — your head! That's where many insects, such as this tiger beetle, have most of their mouthparts.

Insects usually have a pair of hard upper jaws with teeth for biting and chewing and a pair of lower jaws for chewing and holding food. Many insects also have lips. They use their lips to help taste food and guide it inside their bodies. And on either side of the lips and lower jaws, there can be antennalike parts called palps that taste or smell food before it's gobbled up.

The shape and form of an insect's mouthparts depend on what it eats. There are two basic types of mouthparts: chewing and sucking.

Insects such as grasshoppers are chewers. Their jaws cut and grind solid food. Then the lower jaws and lips push the ground-up food inside.

A butterfly is one insect that doesn't chew. It sucks up liquid food instead, through a thin, strawlike tube called a proboscis [pro-BOSS-iss]. It can be longer than the insect's whole body.

The skipper you see here is using its proboscis to sip nectar from a flower. When the skipper has finished feeding, the proboscis will coil up beneath the head, out of the way.

Skipper

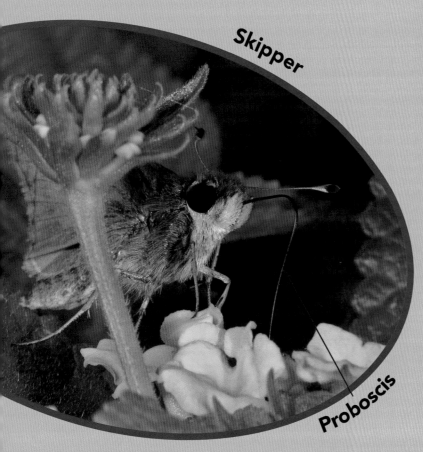

Proboscis

Buggy Bit

A grasshopper uses its palps to make sure a plant is okay to eat.

Eyes

Buggy Bit

Each of the dragonfly's compound eyes has up to 30 000 lenses.

Most insects have two kinds of eyes — compound and simple. The compound eyes take up much of the head. Bulging out on either side, they allow the insects to see in several directions. The eyes receive hundreds or thousands of images because they're each made of hundreds or thousands of lenses. Ordinary houseflies, for instance, have about 4000 lenses in each compound eye. You have only one lens in each of your eyes.

Many insects also have up to three simple eyes, often set between their compound eyes. Each simple eye is small and has just one lens, but it is especially sensitive to light.

Insects can spot movement very well. That's what helps flies avoid flyswatters. Insects can also see the location and form of things and some colors, especially blues. But most insects rely more on their other senses, such as touch, smell and sound.

On the dragonfly, notice the three small simple eyes between the two huge compound eyes. The dragonfly uses its sense of sight more than many other insects do. Its eyesight is among the best in the insect world. The gad fly, however, is one insect that has no simple eyes.

Gad fly

18

Dragonfly

Antennae

A number of tiny segments make up each antenna. Check out this beetle, called a locust borer. You can see the segments in each of its antenna. Insect antennae may be long or short, thick or thin, wide or narrow. Some look like bristles.

Almost all adult insects have two antennae. So do many of their young. The antennae are usually close to the insects' eyes and can turn in all directions.

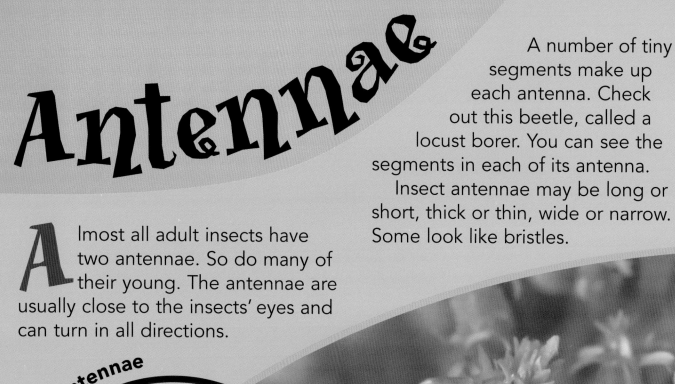

Moth antennae

Others are like feathers or combs. Their size and shape are often related to their use. The feathery antennae of male mosquitoes can detect the humming wings of female mosquitoes. Cockroaches use their long, narrow antennae to feel things. And sharp spines along the antennae of some young water beetles help to break up prey.

Many insects depend on their antennae to detect odors. A keen sense of smell helps many moths find mates. It can also help insects find food. Honeybees, for instance, use their antennae when searching for flowers that are rich with nectar.

Buggy Bit

Locust borers belong to the long-horned beetle family, known for their l-o-n-g antennae.

Locust borer beetle

Hair

Some insects are hairy! Others have just a little body hair. The hairs often sense motion in whatever the insects are standing on. For example, the hair on water striders — insects that walk on water — can detect the ripples made by leaves landing on a pond.

Hairs also sense movement in what's around the insect, even air. Faint puffs of air on the hair of a cockroach's back end, for example, make the insect take off fast.

Insects have other uses for hair, too. Fringes of hair on the wings of small insects make the wings bigger and better for flying. Some caterpillars are covered with poison-filled hairs that can harm predators. And when hairs on the heads of young mosquitoes beat the water, they cause floating food to flow toward them.

Many bees are hairy, as this close-up shows. Pollen from flowers sticks to the hairs. Comblike hairs on the bees' back legs scrape the pollen into "baskets" made of other leg hairs. The bees then carry the pollen to feed their young.

Buggy Bit

The tiny leg hairs of bees can hold large balls of pollen. Note the orange-colored ball in this picture.

Bee

Signals

Finding mates in a big world can be hard for small animals. That's why many insects send signals saying, "Here I am!" Some male grasshoppers scrape their wings together to make sounds. Others scrape their wings with their back legs. Each kind, or species, of grasshopper creates its own "song" to attract females of the same species.

To hear these sound signals, some insects have eardrums. You can spot the eardrum, called a tympanum (TIM-puh-num), on this grasshopper. It has one eardrum on either side of its abdomen. Other grasshopper species have eardrums on their legs.

Cicadas (sih-KAY-duhs) also send sound signals. The males have drumlike tissues on their abdomens. Using their muscles to push these tissues in and out, they can make loud "music." It's among the loudest insect music on Earth.

Other insects use light instead of sound as signals. Many fireflies have light-making organs near the end of their abdomens. After dark, male fireflies in the air flash signals to females on the ground. Each species uses its own flash code. When a female flashes back, a male of her species flies down to her.

Grasshopper tympanum

24

Grasshopper

Eggs

Buggy Bit

A female praying mantis can spend hours making and filling a single egg case.

Insects start life inside eggs. Most of the eggs have two shells: a tough outer one and a softer inner one. But the eggs vary widely in texture, color and shape. The stink bug eggs shown here are shaped like barrels.

A few insects, such as some aphids, have eggs that develop inside their mothers' bodies. The aphids then give birth to live young. But most insects lay their eggs, and the young hatch from them. The females often search for places where the eggs will be safe. Fruit flies, for example, hide their eggs inside fruit. Grasshoppers lay theirs in soil.

Some insects go even further to protect their eggs. Praying mantises make foamy cases that shelter eggs from wind and rain. Moths may cover their eggs with stinging hairs gathered from shed exoskeletons. Predators beware! And lacewings lay eggs on top of the threadlike "stems" they make. That keeps the first hatchlings from eating the rest of the eggs — they don't ever climb up the stems.

A few insects care for their eggs until they hatch. A male giant water bug carries about a hundred eggs on his back. He takes them to the water's surface for air from time to time and guards them from predators.

When insects hatch, some simply push open lidlike caps on their eggs. But many have to hammer their way out, often with their heads. Others use an egg burster, a special body part that pierces the shell then disappears during the insect's first molt. Usually just one insect emerges from each egg. But a single egg laid by some wasps can produce as many as 1000 new wasps!

Stink bug eggs

Praying mantis egg case

Metamorphosis

Most insects don't just get bigger as they get older. Their bodies go through a change in form and function called metamorphosis [met-uh-MORE-fuh-sis]. Grasshoppers, aphids and praying mantises are a few of the insects that have a gradual metamorphosis. The young, called a nymph [nimf], usually looks a lot like the adult. Changes in a nymph happen gradually. Wings, for example, look like small pads at first. They grow and develop into full-sized working wings after the last molt when the nymph turns into an adult.

Beetles, flies, bees and butterflies are examples of insects that experience complete metamorphosis. The young, called a larva, seldom looks like the adult. Changes in the larva usually happen suddenly. After the final molt, the larva enters a pupa stage, where body parts break down and regroup as an adult body. When the insect emerges from the pupa stage as an adult, it often lives only a short time. Its main purpose is to mate and lay eggs.

A mosquito goes through a complete metamorphosis. The larva lives and feeds in water. It moves around the water during the pupa stage, but it doesn't eat. The mosquito starts feeding again when it becomes an adult.

Mosquito larva

Mosquito pupa

Buggy Bit
Some mosquitoes go through a complete metamorphosis in only four days.

Mosquito adult emerging from pupa

Colors

Few other animals are more colorful than insects. Their bright colors and patterns often help them avoid being eaten. For example, predators come to learn that the yellow and black stripes on a bee mean there's a stinger, too. Some insects draw attention to their warning colors by swaying back and forth.

Bright colors can also fool predators. Grasshoppers sometimes flash yellow and black colors as they fly off. Predators chasing them then hunt for yellow and black prey.

As the grasshoppers land, they fold their front wings to hide these colors. Poof! It's as if the insects have disappeared.

Color can also help insects blend in with their backgrounds. White moths, for example, can barely be seen when they rest on white flowers. The green leafhopper shown here looks like part of a plant. There are even caterpillars that are colored like bird droppings on a branch. Unless the caterpillars move, you would never guess they were there.

Leafhopper

Buggy Bit

Scarlet wings and black spots on ladybugs signal a bad taste.

Ladybug

Shapes

Buggy Bit

The veins on a katydid's wings look just like the veins on a leaf.

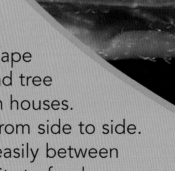

Most insects have bodies that are long and narrow. And their right and left sides usually look alike.

A few insects, however, have odd shapes to help them hide from hungry predators. Treehoppers, for example, can look like the thorns that grow along some plant stems. Katydids can be shaped like leaves. Predators have a hard time spotting these insects among bushes and trees.

Being raised and rounded can also protect insects. This shape makes many beetles, such as ladybugs, hard to grab.

The bodies of cockroaches are flattened, as though they've been slightly squashed. Their shape lets them creep under stones and tree bark — or under closed doors in houses.

Fleas are also flattened, but from side to side. This body shape lets them slip easily between the hairs of cats, dogs and rabbits to feed.

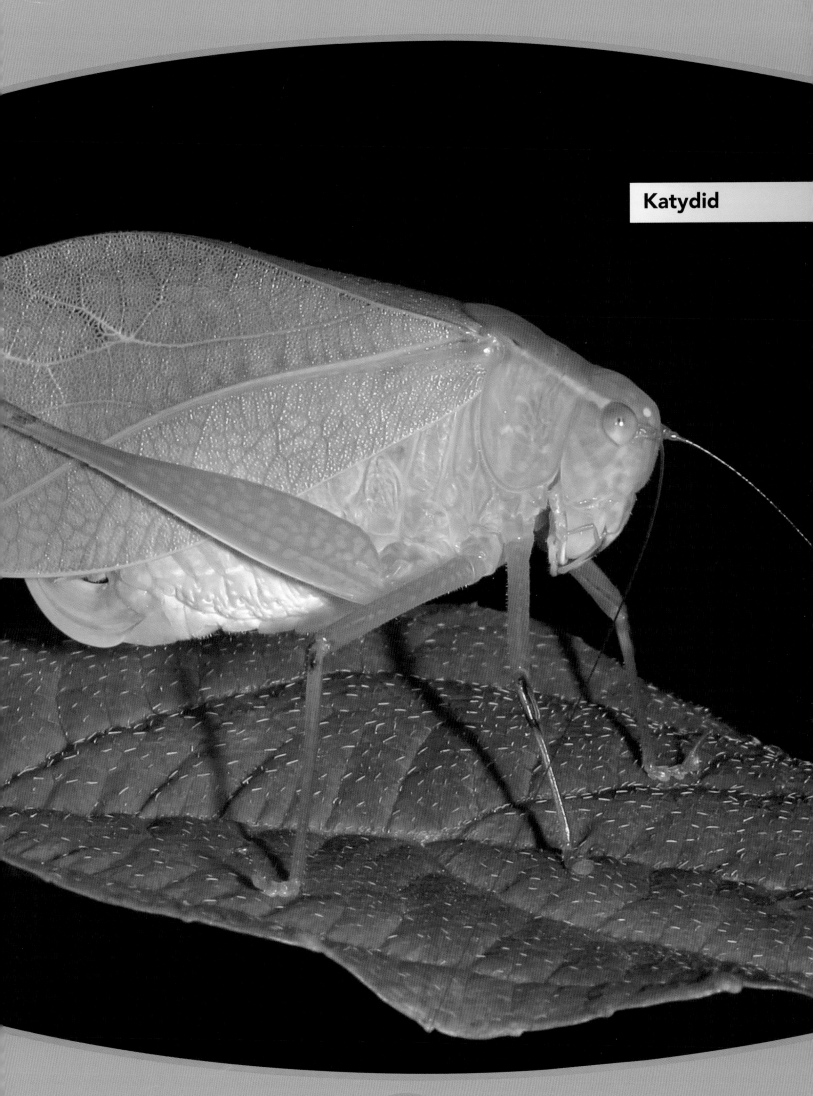

Weapons

Buggy Bit

Female earwigs sometimes use pincers to defend their young from big spiders.

When threatened, some insects fight back. And many have special weapons for the job. The earwig has pincers on its hind end to pinch ants and other attackers. It can also squirt a bad-smelling liquid.

Bombardier beetles squirt their predators, too. The beetles aim their back ends and fire a boiling-hot spray at spiders, mice and toads. The noise and the spray startle the predators. The spray alone can sting or make them sick.

Many bees and wasps depend on sharp stingers to defend themselves and their nests. The stinger injects a poisonous liquid. Long ago, stingers were egg-laying tools, so only the females have them. A wasp or a bumblebee can sting several times, but a honeybee can sting only once. Its stinger has a barbed end that gets stuck in the victim and left there.

Other insects, such as some moths, flash the eyelike markings on their hind wings to scare predators, including small birds. Because these "eyes" seem to belong to an owl or other animal that might eat the birds, they avoid the insects.

Wasp stinger

Earwig

Size

Buggy Bit

You know how small ants are, so think how tiny the green aphids in this picture must be.

Insects vary widely in size, but they're all little. The smallest is no bigger than the dot at the end of this sentence.

Being small can cause big problems. When insects molt, they can dry out quickly and die. Getting wet can also be a problem. If raindrops drench a tiny insect, it has to struggle to free itself from the water or drown.

But the advantages to being little are great. Insects are strong because their muscles are large compared to the size of their bodies. So an ant can carry fifty times its weight, while you can only lift something your own weight.

Safety is another advantage of being small. Even insects that don't fly can fall from almost any height without getting injured. Their size and weight are so slight that they drop slowly through the air and land lightly.

Being tiny also means it's easier to find places to live. Some insects crawl under stones or beneath tree bark. Some spend their whole lives inside nuts. Because they're small, insects can hide almost anywhere to escape predators or extreme temperatures.

As well, insects don't need much food to survive. A single small seed can feed a little insect for life.

Ant with aphids

Success

Earth is an insect planet. At any moment, ten million million million insects live here. Don't believe it? One colony of termites can have millions of members. And a swarm of dragonflies can be so large it takes days to pass a single tree.

Insects are the most common animals, and they're also the most successful. They've existed for about 400 million years, and they live in every country.

Being able to fly means insects can easily find places to feed, lay eggs and escape their enemies. And it helps if they go through a complete metamorphosis, as more than half the insect species do. During metamorphosis, the larva and adult can live in different places, so their chances of finding food are better.

Although some insects spread deadly diseases, such as malaria, much life on Earth could not survive without insects. They are important food for many other animals, such as fish, reptiles, birds — and even people in some countries. Some insects help pollinate plants so that new plants can grow. And many insects get rid of dead animals and body wastes, enriching the soil in the process.

The insects in this book are just a few of the thousands of insect species that might appear in your backyard. They remind us how awesome the world of insects really is.

Buggy Bit

Billions of cicadas can appear in a city at one time.

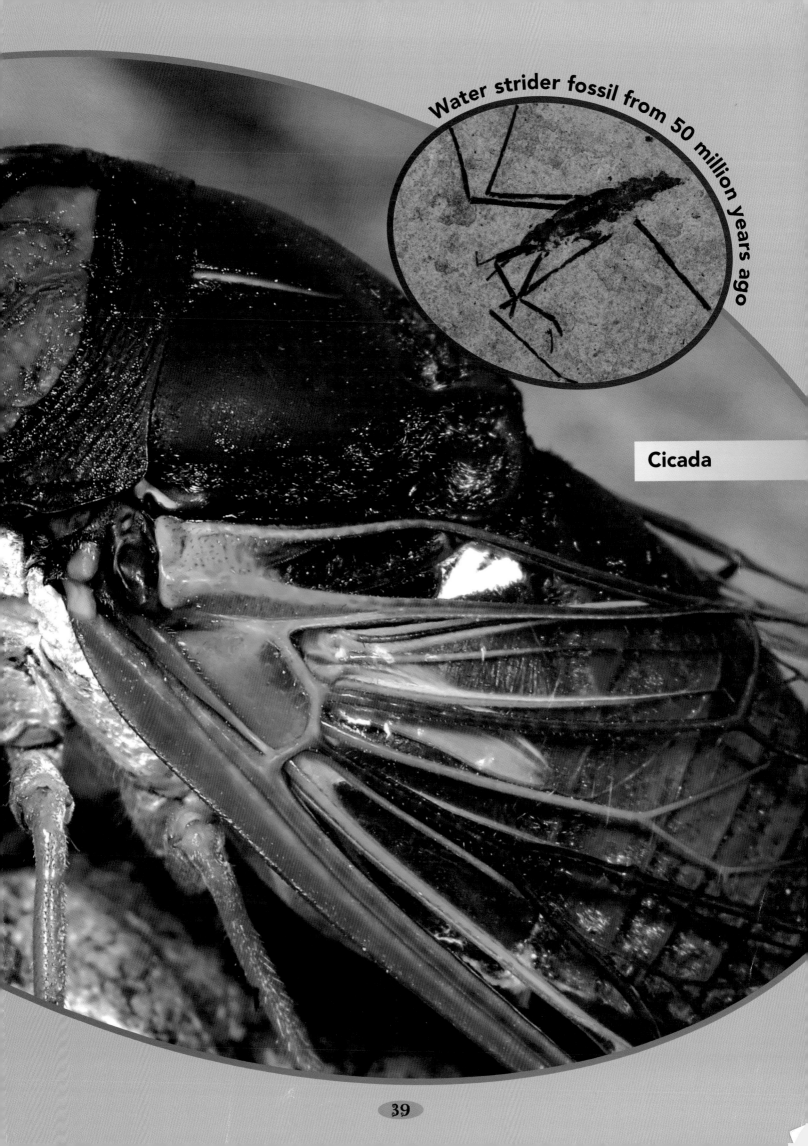

Water strider fossil from 50 million years ago

Cicada

Glossary

abdomen: rear section of an insect's three body sections

antennae: sensors on the head of an insect

exoskeleton: strong material that covers an insect's body

metamorphosis: change in the form and function of an insect's body

molt: shedding of an insect's outer covering, or exoskeleton

nectar: sugary liquid made by flowers

pollen: fertilizing powder made by flowers

predators: animals that kill and eat other animals

prey: animals that are food for other animals

species: kind of insect

thorax: middle section of an insect's three body sections

Index

Use this index to learn more about the insects you find. Numbers in **bold** indicate photos.